Keeping, raising and training horses naturally

The horse book for more pleasure in riding and a close bond with your horse - incl. health guide, ground work, lunging and horse games

Paula Meyerhoff

CONTENTS

What it will be about

In this guide, I would like to give you an insight into keeping, raising and training your horse as a partner. The focus will be on the factor of natural handling. Basic theoretical knowledge will be conveyed with corresponding practical suggestions. Meanwhile, topics such as communication between humans and horses and species-appropriate husbandry will be addressed. Newcomers to the field of riding will gain an extensive insight into the mindset of the four-legged friends and equestrian "know-how". Experienced riders who are already taking their horse to competitions will also find everything they need, from a change of scenery in training to dressage lessons.

When working with young horses, the subject of training is dealt with extensively.

I do not prescribe how to ride "correctly" or "incorrectly". This guide is merely a recommendation on how to deal with horses in a manner appropriate to their species. I want to convey how you can encourage horses without forcing them to do anything unnatural, and how you can spend time with them alongside riding.

The overriding aim of all topics should be the enjoyment of riding and harmony with the horse as a partner.

Understanding the horse as an animal

To be able to work with horses, you first have to understand them. They may not speak our language, but they express themselves very clearly. It used to be assumed that horses follow a stimulus-response pattern, but we soon realized that they are very capable of thinking and do so in a very individual way. We humans can react to what they think if we interpret a horse's behavior correctly. You can understand them by fundamentally accepting them.

Horses are flight animals and are therefore always alert and curious when they are not in a safe environment or herd. They notice immediately if a situation could become dangerous. This often seems amusing if it is just a branch lying on the road, for example. But anything that seems unusual could turn into a danger. With this prior knowledge, situations can be mitigated and avoided in advance by putting ourselves in the horse's shoes.

Horses show their mood through sounds, touch and changes in posture. The position of the ears clearly shows how a horse is feeling or where its attention is. But you can also see in the horse's eyes, as in those of humans, what state of mind it is in.

If you observe horses in a herd, you can quickly determine who is the alpha dog and who is the "underdog", i.e. the lower-ranking animal. In a herd of horses, there is often a fight over the hierarchy. However, it is not just a question of who has more strength. Horses also pay attention to behavioral experiences and social skills. For people who want to work with horses, knowledge of the hierarchy is extremely important, because horses also test rank in humans and this can lead to dangerous situations in an emergency. You should therefore always pay attention to how you come across to a horse.

Horses don't necessarily want to be the boss either. Even if a high-ranking position is attractive, they often seek safety and protection from conspecifics as well as humans. For example, if a horse lies down in the presence of a human, this is a great sign of trust, as it then feels safe enough to relinquish observation of its surroundings and make itself "vulnerable".

A natural and healthy basis for husbandry

All of the horse's needs should be respected in the way it is kept. For their physical and mental health, they need light, air, companions and exercise. Horses are running animals and move around in nature for up to 16 hours a day. That's why the way they are kept should above all allow movement. Keeping a horse in a box all day is practical because it is always available, easy to feed and usually clean, but it is cruel to animals. This is why classic stall keeping must guarantee sufficient access to the paddock with the opportunity for social contact with "buddies".

If a horse has too little exercise, boredom is quickly reflected in bad habits such as bucking and weaving. When bucking, the animal sets its teeth on a horizontal object, tenses its lower neck muscles and draws air into the gullet, producing a belching sound. Weaving is characterized by the animals swinging from one front leg to the other and spreading their legs apart. In most cases, the head is also swiveled or stretched upwards. Neither behavioral disorder is physically harmful, but they show us that they are under psychological stress.

To make stabling as comfortable as possible, it is advisable to adapt the stall to the needs of the horse. With as much light, air and room to move as possible, ideally even an adjoining paddock, the stall will be more species-appropriate. Above all, the size of the box should be appropriate for the horse's body size.

Horses feel most comfortable in a loose or open stable. They can get enough exercise and, above all, have contact with their fellow horses.

THE FEEDING

In addition to sufficient exercise, a balanced diet is also part of species-appropriate husbandry. This does not mean that only the most expensive or the most 'exquisite' food is best.

With the right knowledge about the horse's physique, requirements and digestion, you have a good basis for putting together the right feed for your horse. For horses with health problems or sport horses, it is advisable to seek professional advice. Straw, hay, silage (green fodder preserved by fermentation) or grass form the basis of a balanced diet. They provide fiber, which removes harmful substances from the digestive system, generally supports it and cleanses the intestines. A horse should receive approx. 1.5 kg of roughage per 100 kg of weight per day. For a 700 kg animal, for example, this would be 10.5 kg of hay, grass etc. per day.

In addition to roughage, concentrated feed can be fed, depending on how much a horse is in training. If the horse does not get enough energy from the roughage, it can be supplemented with various mueslis or pellets. These contain a lot of grain, oil, vitamins, minerals and trace elements such as selenium or zinc. Sport horses are usually also given oats. For decades, it has been the energy supplier that everyone counts on, and horses love it. Oils, such as those obtained from linseed, can support a horse's stamina. Racehorses are usually given additional mineral feed that contains a lot of iron, selenium and copper to ensure that they are adequately supported in their supply of nutrients. For mares that are suckling their foals, there is special compound feed that is rich in protein to provide them with sufficient nutrients.

When foals are weaned from their mother's milk, they also need more protein, which must be fed to them.

Bread, carrots, apples, bananas and the like can add variety to the diet. But caution is advised: The sugar and yeast in bread are harmful in excess, which is why everything should only be fed in small quantities.

The horse's stomach is small. It is therefore important to ensure that everything is fed in small quantities regularly throughout the day and not all at once. It is ideal if horses can graze in a paddock during the day so that a large part of the roughage is already covered in addition to the concentrated feed.

HEALTH - THE BE-ALL AND END-ALL

You have to take great responsibility for horses. Especially when it comes to the health of the four-legged friends. Everyday grooming in particular helps to keep them healthy. The horse is not only groomed, but also checked for ticks, small wounds or areas that are too warm. This can prevent serious diseases that can be transmitted by ticks, for example. Especially after a horse has been in the paddock or walked through tall grass, it should be thoroughly checked for ticks. If you notice an open wound during grooming, clean it carefully beforehand. An antiseptic (disinfectant) ointment, such as iodine ointment, can then be applied. If warm spots are noticed, they should definitely be observed. If the area swells, for example, this may be a sign of tendon damage. A vet should definitely examine the area.

Many owners are afraid of overlooking possible symptoms and not taking appropriate action in time. It is therefore important to be informed about the most common symptoms, their consequences and treatment.

POISONOUS PLANTS

To avoid poisoning, it is important to check the paddock regularly. Plants that are harmful to horses can always grow there. These include **aconite and monkshood,** both of which are easily recognized by their bright color and hat-shaped flowers. The **yew is** one of the most poisonous plants for horses. It is a coniferous tree that is often found in bush form. In spring, it can be easily recognized by its round red fruits. Another example is **ragwort,** which is often found in meadows. It is approx. 30 to 100 cm high and the elongated stalks are topped with flowers about 2 cm in size and around 13 yellow leaves. The **sycamore**, **St. John's wort**, **false acacia**, **boxwood** and many **decorative plants and flowers are also** poisonous to four-legged friends.

Poisoning by plants can occur immediately or only after days or weeks. Typical symptoms are sweating, breathing problems, trembling, foaming at the mouth, diarrhea and colic.

COLIC - RED ALERT

Colic is probably what most riders fear, as this condition can be a matter of life and death. The term colic is a collective term for any kind of pain in the horse's abdomen. In most cases, colic is the result of an intestinal cramp. This occurs due to disturbances in the intestines. When there is a disturbance, the intestinal movement increases and other parts cramp up until the intestine no longer works. As a result, the horse can no longer defecate and the intestine becomes blocked. Various types of colic can develop in this way. One example would be the colic of the stool. It occurs when we feed incorrectly. Too much grain and sugar, too little roughage or simply too much at once damage the intestines and lead to constipation.

Feed is also the trigger for flatulence or gas colic. This will occur, for example, if horses are not grazed slowly in spring and eat fresh grass from one day to the next. Young grass is very high in sugar and protein. If horses eat too much of this at once during their first walk on green pasture, this leads to disturbances in the bacterial balance, as so many nutrients cannot be utilized quickly enough. Gas is produced, which then expands the intestines because it cannot escape.

Probably the worst type of colic occurs when the intestine becomes knotted. This interrupts the blood supply, causing the tissue to die. If the horse does not receive an operation quickly enough, it is doomed.

Lighter forms of colic are not operated on straight away; treatment by the vet in the stable is often sufficient. The vet should be called immediately if you notice the following symptoms: Restlessness, listlessness, repeatedly looking at the abdomen as well as kicking at the abdomen, rolling, repeatedly lying down and getting up again, lying down for long periods at unusual times and restless breathing. If colic is suspected, the vet should be contacted immediately. Until the vet arrives, it is important to provide first aid by taking the PAT values (pulse, respiration, temperature). Normally, these are 28 to 40 pulses and 8 to 16 breaths per minute as well as a body temperature of between 37.5 and 38.3 degrees Celsius.

It is important to prevent any feed intake. It is best to move the horse from the ground in an indoor arena so that it has the opportunity to roll around at any time. If the horse remains lying down, it should be motivated to stand up. Only if the pulse is 60 or higher is it not advisable to move the horse, as this can lead to a collapse. In general, keep calm and pay attention to the horse's behavior until the vet arrives.

THE VET CHECK

Caring for and keeping horses with care and in a species-appropriate manner is more than half the battle in maintaining their health. However, some veterinary examinations are advisable.

In general, a purchase inspection should be carried out when buying a horse. As with cars, there is also an MOT for four-legged friends, which checks everything once. A purchase inspection is practically a small MOT. The buyer decides exactly what is checked. Serious illnesses or injuries should be identified. In the small MOT, the skin and coat are checked in advance, the heart and lungs are listened to and the pulse, breathing rate and temperature are taken. The eyes, respiratory and nervous system, heart, mouth and the horse's apples are then examined for abnormalities. The musculoskeletal system is also checked. The back is checked by palpation and the legs are inspected by stretching. By having the horse trot forward, the vet can determine whether the animal is walking without problems or pain. After exercise, the pulse and breathing are checked repeatedly to diagnose any coughing or differences in breathing sounds.

It is also advisable to have a blood count done if you do not know the seller. This can reveal whether the animal has been given painkillers or other medication.

In addition to the minor examinations mentioned above, X-rays are also taken at the major MOT. As standard, this includes 10 x-rays of the legs to take a closer look at the hooves, fetlocks and hocks. Depending on which abnormalities have already been seen in the horse for sale, related areas should also be x-rayed. The vet will use the results of the examination to draw up a report in which various classes of findings are listed. A finding does not necessarily mean that the horse is ill. Depending on the class, the abnormalities should be monitored further during routine visits and any necessary treatment carried out.

In order to immunize a horse against the most common infectious diseases, certain vaccinations should be given. Which vaccination is administered, when and how often depends on the animal. Foals should only be vaccinated after they are five months old, as they do not yet produce the substances required for vaccination. During this time, it is passively immune due to antibodies contained in the mother's milk. The way the horse is kept, the specifications of breeding associations and the intended use of the horse also determine what and how it is vaccinated. Vaccinations are generally given against tetanus (tetanus), equine distemper (inflammation of the arteries), equine influenza (influenza disease) and also against the recently emerged herpes virus (nerve damage).

Vaccinations are most effective when the entire herd of a stable is vaccinated at the same time. Just like the worming treatment, which rids the horse of any worms it may have picked up while grazing. It does not fulfill its purpose if it is not administered to all the horses in a stable at the same time.

The education

There are many things that horses should learn so that they can be handled without danger. Horses like to be rough with other horses. Nipping and nudging is part of herd life. However, playful teasing can be dangerous for humans, as the animals are much bigger and stronger. Horses are open-minded animals that include us in their social behavior. They have to learn where the differences lie compared to their conspecifics. Good behavior should therefore be taught from foal age. This includes not only earning respect, but also building trust. Even as foals, horses should allow themselves to be touched everywhere. Like us humans, however, they also have places that tickle. They should learn that it does not immediately mean that they have to "tickle back", but that they should tolerate being touched. This also makes work easier for the vet or farrier.

You should make your position in the hierarchy clear at all times, because horses always like to test where they stand. This can be recognized by snapping, pushing and jostling. Behaviors such as pushing or nudging humans often appear to be "cute", but the horse sees humans as lower-ranking animals at such times. The behavior should therefore always be analyzed carefully. Small power games are part of it, but they should be reacted to consistently at all times.

A firm "no" or something similar is usually enough. If not, then you should be much louder. If there is still no reaction, a threatening gesture, a tug on the lead rope or a small slap can help. If the animal reacts and stops being naughty, it should be praised. Our posture is often enough to ensure that a horse doesn't test us so often by acting calmly but clearly and confidently.

You should react to any situation in a controlled and calm manner. Stress only hinders learning. Animals should also not be overtaxed. They can quickly become mentally exhausted and need some time out to process new impressions. The timing of training sessions should therefore not only be adapted to the horse, but also to the content.

Standing still is an important exercise in training. As horses are running animals, many find it difficult to stand still. However, this is the basis for many exercises and everyday tasks to run smoothly. A horse needs to stand still at the vet or farrier, when grooming, saddling or mounting. The "Stand!" command should therefore be taught extensively from an early age. Be it when leading, tying or scratching, standing still should become a matter of course. Practicing while tying up is particularly useful if there is another horse next to you that can already stand still. When practising while leading, make sure that the horse understands which position it should be in. Its shoulder should be close to that of the human. Once a horse has understood this, they usually realize on their own when they are going too fast or too slow, or when they have to stop. The correct position when leading also has something to do with who is the boss at that moment. If the horse is too far forward, the human can no longer exert any influence. In everyday gaits, it is therefore also important to remain attentive and consistent! Especially with young animals.

Training also includes putting on and taking off the bridle and saddle at a certain age. By nature, horses are not familiar with these objects and usually want to get rid of them as quickly as possible. This is why understanding and patience are so important when training. If something doesn't work straight away or the horse doesn't react as described in the books, it's not the end of the world. Every horse reacts differently and takes longer or less time to learn or break the habit.

Although horses are flight animals, they are still curious. If they are afraid of something or even flee, you should allow them to take a closer look at the feared object, which helps horses learn quickly. If the confrontation with unusual objects such as fluttering ribbons, umbrellas or plastic tarpaulins is practiced often, the general fear of unknown things is also reduced. With particularly fearful horses, it often helps if an experienced horse leads the way and shows that there is no danger, because horses, like humans, learn by example. Repetition of what has been learned is important for long-term results, no matter how old the animal is.

IS THERE RIGHT AND WRONG?

No. As just mentioned, every horse thinks differently. Behavioral predictions can generally be followed, but reality always holds surprises. Mistakes are part and parcel of training animals, regardless of whether they are made by humans or animals.

Engage, motivate and teach horses

Horses never get bored in the wild. They are busy with their conspecifics, foraging for food and observing their surroundings to protect the herd. They should therefore be offered sufficient activity and variety.

MOTIVATION THROUGH VARIETY

Young horses in particular get bored quickly and then become unfocused. Understandably, we don't want to hear the same news every day. New stimuli should therefore be created again and again. The best way to do this is in nature. On walks or rides, you often encounter situations that are unfamiliar. Be it a fallen tree or a pile of stones that wasn't there last time.

HORSE GAMES

Horses have a strong play instinct by nature. Behavioral scientists claim that it is even a sign of higher intelligence and keeps them fit. Horses can not only play in the herd, but we humans can also have fun with them. Lazy and sleepy horses can be given back the joy of movement and annoying horses become more balanced. In addition, humans and animals get to know each other better and trust is strengthened.

Simple objects make it easy to play. An exercise ball can be sniffed, nudged or kicked in the hall, on the field or on a meadow. You can also play with food. With a few treats or carrots in your pocket, you can "fool around" with horses and also play catch.

However, it should always be borne in mind that horses can also become overconfident. A certain amount of caution should therefore always be exercised.

GROUND WORK

Ground work, as the name suggests, refers to working with the horse from the ground.

It provides variety in everyday riding and is the perfect solution for horses that cannot be ridden for short or long periods of time. The horse is gently exercised and body control is improved. In addition to the exercise and variety factor, working from the ground strengthens confidence and reassures the horse that it can rely on humans. This also makes it much easier and more enjoyable to teach horses new things.

A good example is backing up. You can prepare the horse for this dressage lesson perfectly from the ground. Stand in front of the horse so that you are looking at it. With your body confidently erect, you now approach the animal. Ideally, the horse will move backwards without you touching it. If not, then a gentle touch on the chest and the signal word "Back" is usually enough. After a few passes, the exercise will also work without touching. Basically, any exercise can be tried out in advance using ground work. Be it walking through water, running over tarpaulins, dressage exercises or cavaletti work. From the ground, horses are not confronted alone, but always have a caregiver next to them. And that's what it's all about - mastering different challenges together.

If an exercise works, whether at the first attempt or after prolonged trial and error, it is important to praise it extensively. However, this should not always be done with a treat. Stroking between the eyes is also a reward. A calm voice also has a rewarding effect. Otherwise, it will happen in no time at all and the horse will start to perform tasks without being asked in order to get treats. This type of begging should be avoided in the first place.

Clicker training

Another type of reward is the clicker. This is better known from dog training, but it can be used with any animal. The clicker is a small device containing a clicker frog. If you press it, you hear the typical click sound. You train a horse by pressing the clicker once after successfully completing an exercise and then immediately giving a treat. This is practiced until the horse has understood the click sound as praise. One advantage of clicking is that you can also praise from a certain distance.

Clicking can be combined with working with the target stick. This is a stick with a ball at the tip. When the horse touches it with its nose, it is praised. The animal associates something positive with the stick. The aim is to use the target stick to introduce horses to unfamiliar things.

Cavaletti work

Working with cavalettis is a mindfulness exercise and is practical when the horse is young if you intend to work on jumps later on. First and foremost, however, it gymnasticizes every horse and every rider, as it requires a firm seat. Nothing works without balance. Cavalettis are poles that are about 3 meters long. They are placed on the ground or set up to form obstacles 40 to 80 centimetres high. They can be set up in a variety of ways.

However, there are usually several poles in a row. A horse should first get a feel for how best to walk over them. To do this, it should only be led over them at the beginning of the work with cavalettis. Once the horse seems more sure-footed, you can start to ride over them at a walk. If this also works without any problems, you can move on to trotting and later galloping.

Above all, this strengthens the feeling for the right rhythm. Cavaletti training is therefore also recommended from time to time for riders who specialize in dressage.

The horse playground

You can do even more with poles than just building small jumps. The horse playground is a little less about tact than working with cavalettis. The main focus here is on having fun. Nevertheless, concentration is also required. If something goes wrong, it should not be punished. After all, the horse is learning new things and should also enjoy them. Mistakes are also part of playing.

A small maze or square can be constructed from poles in just a few simple steps, through which the four-legged friends can be led. This is all about flexibility and sure-footedness. Tight bends are not so easy for horses. They have to shift their balance backwards. This exercise is very practical for younger horses that are being prepared for riding and will pay dividends later on. The balance of horses can also be trained by building an "L" out of poles. The horse should be guided forwards and backwards through this. This requires concentration and coordination from both partners.

If you have a few metal or plastic barrels lying around, these can be used for a barrel slalom. They can be put together in any shape. Initially, you should make sure that there is enough space between the barrels. This can then be reduced over time to increase the level of difficulty. In addition to the playful aspect, the result is that the horse becomes more flexible.

Courage is required when working with car tires. If you have old tires, these can also be used when playing. This is particularly good for building trust, as for most horses it will be their first encounter with this strange object. So the first thing to do is to let the horse sniff it out. Once the horse is familiar with the tire and seems relaxed, it can be led further towards it until it possibly places a front hoof in it. If not, you can also help a little by lifting the leg and placing it slowly in the hoop. If this is successful, it should be praised extensively. With consistent training, you can work towards getting the horse to stand with all four legs in a hoop at the same time. This exercise is particularly useful if the legs need to be cooled in buckets of water due to illness, for example.

But there are also many other ways to develop a horse playground. All you need is creativity.

Lunging

When lunging, you let the horse walk a circle around you on a lunge line (approx. 9 meters long). The horse can wear a bridle without reins or a cavesson. This is a bridle that is constructed like a typical noseband, only it acts on the nose bone and not via the mouth. If you use a bridle with a bit, the use of lunging goggles is recommended. Lunging goggles are a short strap, usually made of leather, to which carabiners are attached at both ends. These are hooked onto the bit rings from below. The lunge line is attached to a third carabiner in the middle of the strap. By using lunging goggles, the effect of the lunge line is not only distributed on one side, but evenly on both sides of the bit.

A lunging girth with auxiliary reins can be used to help horses stretch and collect. This is placed on the withers like a saddle. A number of rings are attached to it so that the auxiliary reins can be attached. One example would be the triangular reins. They consist of 2 long straps that are attached to the lowest girth point and then run between the front legs to the bit rings. There they are pulled through and run to the right and left of the horse to the rings, where they are fastened again. A triangle is formed between the bit ring and the girth. They take over the rider's guiding rein fist and are only intended to support stretching and contact. A whip is also part of the basic equipment required for lunging. It is used to frame the horse. It should always be directed just behind the hindquarters for forward propulsion. A triangle is formed between the rider, the horse's head and hindquarters. The whip can be swung to intensify the drive. To slow down the pace, it can be directed further back so that the triangle opens up and the horse is given space to the rear.

Lunging is particularly suitable as a change in the training program. However, it also offers a good alternative if the rider is unable to work the horse from above for health reasons, for example, or if the horse cannot be ridden. In general, lunging supports concentration, fitness and coordination as well as confidence. It is also useful for seat training and beginner lessons. The rider can pay full attention to their seat without having to concentrate 100 percent on the speed or direction in which they are riding. Working on the lunge line also makes it more comfortable for the instructor. He can intervene better and focus more on the student's seat.

It is important to remember that the sides must be changed regularly, as the horse only moves in one direction when lunging. You should also think about uniformity here.

Horsemanship

Horsemanship encompasses the general art of riding and the fair treatment of horses. It therefore begins as soon as you start to deal with the animal.

The term was made famous by Pat Parelli and Monty Roberts, both former Ro-deo riders. The aim is to establish a connection with the horse and not to demand a performance that the horse cannot deliver. This can only be achieved with clear rules and fair communication. Correct training is characterized by small steps that build on each other.

PAT PARELLI - NATURAL HORSE-MANSHIP

Natural horsemanship according to Pat Parelli is primarily about training people to understand the horse's behavior as well as possible. Above all, working with the horse requires mutual trust, respect and free communication, taking into account the different characters of the horses. This is described by the term "horsenality". Even among horses, there are extroverted and introverted animals. Different types of horses require different ways of handling. Some exercises may have to be approached completely differently for the horse to understand the human at all. A distinction is made between "left brain" and "right brain" horses. Left-brain horses are courageous, dominant and calm, while right-brain horses tend to be suspicious, reserved and fearful.

A further step in the analysis of "horsenality" is to find out whether a horse is introverted, i.e. with little urge to move forward, or extroverted, with a lot of energy and urge to move . This leads to the following conclusion: a horse that is "left brain, extroverted" needs a lot of variety and learns quickly. If the horse is "left brain, introverted", it knows exactly what it wants and is usually not prepared to do more. "Right brain, extroverted" is a horse that quickly becomes anxious and questions everything. A horse that is reserved and calm belongs to the "right brain, introverted" category. The behavior that humans choose when dealing with a horse should be adapted according to the category, e.g. dominant or confidence-inspiring. This is the only way to ensure fair and free communication.

There are also the "Seven Games according to Parelli". These are also designed to optimize communication between humans and horses. The games build on each other. However, the first game can always be incorporated in between.

"The Friendly Game" forms the beginning of the game series. The aim is to reassure the horse that you will not hurt it and that it can trust you. The animal is always positively influenced by being stroked. From time to time, however, it is confronted with frightening situations or objects. For example, this could be a saddle pad for a young animal. This is repeatedly placed on the horse's back during stroking, then stroked and taken off again. During this time, the horse should not be tied up, but only held by a rope. The horse must be given the opportunity to move out of the way if necessary. It is also important that the alternation of confrontation and stroking takes place in a constant rhythm. This allows the horse to anticipate the situation. This gives him a sense of security. The aim is for the horse to learn that nothing bad will happen to it in the presence of humans.

Game number two is **"The Porcupine** Game". The aim here is to teach the horse to yield to pressure. This can be used to teach forehand and hindquarters turns on the ground, as well as backing and lowering the head. Let's take the latter as an example: First, light, steady pressure is applied behind the poll with the fingertips. If the horse does not react to this, the pressure is intensified. If nothing happens afterwards, it is increased a little more. If the horse lowers its head, the pressure is immediately and completely removed. The fact that the pressure does not follow is a positive connection for the horse. After a few practice sessions, the horse understands that it should respond to the pressure by giving way.

"The Driving Game" is the third level of the game. It builds directly on the "Porcupine Game". The horse should now learn to yield to humans without touching them. For example, if it is to move backwards, the animal is approached straight on. Ideally, it will go backwards straight away if it has already understood that a certain distance must be maintained. Otherwise, you can help with a hand movement or by swinging a rope. But even then the horse should not be touched. This is practiced until the animal moves backwards when the distance is reduced.

The fourth game is **"The Yo-Yo-Game"** (the yo-yo game). The aim is to send the horse back in a straight line and then reload it. This game should also be played without touching the horse (except for praise).

This is followed by **"The Circling** Game". The horse is lunged for this. The aim is for the horse to maintain the required gait until it is asked to do something else. In the meantime, you should stand in the middle of the circle and not walk along. As soon as the horse parries out of the required gait, it is brought into the circle and sent out again. The horse will quickly understand that it is more comfortable to stay on the circle. If it maintains the correct gait, it is left alone. Cavalettis can also be incorporated on the circle during this exercise to provide variety.

In the **"sideways game",** the horse is first sent away by applying light pressure to the head, then to the hindquarters. This is repeated until the horse aligns itself and moves sideways. It is useful to perform this exercise in front of a wall or fence so that the horse cannot move forward. It is important that the exercise is practiced evenly on both sides of the horse.

The final game is **"The Squeeze Game".** You stand about three meters away from a wall and then ask the horse to run between them. The distance to the wall is then slowly reduced to one meter. The horse should be given a moment to relax after walking through so that it associates this with comfort. This can give you many advantages when loading onto a trailer.

Each of the games is mentally demanding for the horse. Care must therefore be taken not to overtax it too much. Thinking can also be very strenuous.

One of Monty Roberts' special methods is the join-up. Originally an alternative to "breaking", i.e. forcibly breaking in wild mustangs. In a round pen (a fenced-in circular area), the horse moves freely around the trainer, who is in the middle. By sending the horse away using hand signals or throwing a lunge line in the direction of the animal, the trainer wants to make it clear: "If you don't want to come to me, then go away." If the inner ear is directed towards the trainer, he knows that he has the attention of the horse. Because horses are herd animals, after a while they will feel the urge to join someone. By licking its lips, chewing and lowering its head, the horse signals that it is submitting.

If the horse expresses this, the instructor steps slightly in front of the horse to slow it down. The instructor then turns towards the animal's axis at a 45 degree angle with a lowered gaze. This is known as "inviting the horse into the herd". If the horse responds, it approaches the instructor and seeks contact - the so-called join-up. The trainer can now slowly turn towards the horse and stroke it between the eyes beforehand. He can then also scratch the horse all over its body to welcome it. In the wild, horses would first sniff each other and get to know each other. No eye contact is made during the entire process.

The join-up is now followed by the follow-up. If the instructor starts walking, the horse can be expected to follow. The horse sees him as a leader and has submitted.

However, if the animal does not approach the trainer, the trainer can walk back and forth a little while maintaining a passive attitude towards the horse and keeping a sufficient distance. If the horse still does not react, it is sent away again and the game starts all over again.

Natural dressing

For centuries, the horse was seen exclusively as a farm animal. It is often associated with dressage sport and some people question the rider's intentions. Critics often say: "The horse is just a good-looking sporting object that has to perform. If it doesn't, then harsher means are used." Everyone has to decide for themselves what rules they want to follow when working with their four-legged friends. Just because some behavior is questionable doesn't mean that dressage is cruelty to animals. Performing lessons in a test has nothing whatsoever to do with training lessons for the sake of it, such as in the circus. Dressage is the basis of all horse training. The aim is to improve the animal's ability to move and to establish fine communication between rider and horse. The horse is not made for dressage, but dressage is made for the horse. The horse's muscles should be loosened, elasticized and gymnasticized. Only in this way can dressage lessons be mastered successfully and appropriately.

THE TRAINING

For a horse to be willing to work, well-mannered and pleasant to ride, it needs careful training. The training of a horse is based on a scale published by the German Equestrian Federation (FN). This is divided into different phases. Phase one is the familiarization phase, in which rhythm and suppleness are trained.
This means that attention is paid to the evenness of the steps and jumps and that the muscles tense and relax without tension. This phase is followed by the development of pushing power in phase two. Here, work is already being done on a steady, soft connection between the horse's mouth and the rider's hand.

The swing should also be developed. This means that the hindquarters should become more active in order to create an overall forward movement over the back. In phase three, the aim is to develop carrying power. To achieve this, both sides of the horse's body should be trained evenly in order to compensate for the natural crookedness that every horse has. It is also important to build up collection in the final phase. To achieve this, the hindquarters must be trained to step under more. This can be encouraged, for example, by working on tempi changes and the shoulder-in (a form of lateral movements). In some cases, the individual points develop in parallel and overlap the three phases.

By working from the ground and general training, we also work on permeability and balance in addition to the phases. A horse is trained fairly according to this concept. Classical riding theory is based on the needs, individual dispositions and physical requirements of the animal. It should be gymnasticized and strengthened in a balanced way. This requires a rider with fine aids and a balanced seat. The aim is to produce a willing and trusting horse that is ready to perform. This lays the foundation for further training.

Horses can't be taught anything that their nature can't do on its own. They can do every dressage lesson anyway, we just train them to perform a lesson with a specific aid.

THE STRUCTURE OF A SUPPOR-
TIVE RIDING LESSON

We start with the solution phase. It is very important because it forms the basis of the training. Mistakes can already be made here. Too little walk, not enough forward, no hoof beat figures, too tight turns, asking for lessons too early, etc. This is why it is particularly important to pay attention to the horse here. As the name suggests, the horse should loosen up in this phase. This means that the muscles and joints should be warmed up and the circulation should be stimulated.

It starts with a walking phase. It is usually said to be around 10 minutes long, but this varies from horse to horse. A sport horse will warm up more quickly than an older horse. Frequent changes of gait, changes of hand and large curved lines help to avoid overstraining the joints. The time it takes to reach the goal of the release phase varies from horse to horse. You can test the willingness to stretch by "letting the reins out of your hand". You can check whether the horse is standing on the aids by brushing over it (pushing the rein fist forward along the mane ridge). If everything works without the horse breaking out, you can move on to the next phase. In the working phase, all the

points mentioned in the training scale should be achieved.

Uniformity, suppleness, collection, permeability
etc. are tested here. What exactly is to be achieved as a
goal in this phase and to what degree lessons are tested
depends on the performance level of the rider and the
horse. The training objectives should always be adapted to the level of training of both partners. Basically,
the following applies: The contact can be encouraged
by changing the gait and varying the hoof beats. The
collection can be improved with the help of parades
(interplay of weight, leg and rein aids), short turns (the
horse turns 180 degrees around the backhand with the
forehand) and backwards. There are countless maga-
zines and books available to give you more ideas for
training, provide variety and set new goals. You can
also get good tips from experienced riders or trainers.

It is important to take breaks in between. Getting
stuck on one exercise is counterproductive. It tires
both animal and rider and may even cause frustration.
That's why you should take breaks for a few minutes
every now and then during intensive training to relax
and take a deep breath.

Once the work phase has been successfully com-
pleted, do not try anything else. Training should

always end with a positive experience. If something doesn't go as planned, it's not the end of the world. Downs are part of it, otherwise there wouldn't be any ups. In a low, no one should be blamed for something not working out. It's more about insight, recognizing shortcomings and using them to develop further. It is often simply due to the form of the day that something is not right, whether for us or for the animal. Just like humans, horses also have bad days when they don't have enough energy or their heads are already spinning mentally. Mares in particular often have changing tempers. You shouldn't blame the horse or yourself. There is always a new day. At the end of the day, a lesson must be performed that is sure to end in a positive result. Once you are satisfied with this, the relaxation phase begins. The lesson ends with a relaxed light trot and "letting the reins out of the hand". This is followed by a walk phase adapted to the training, in which the horse can stretch forwards and downwards. It should therefore arch its back and actively step under with its hindquarters so that it can walk freely from the shoulder.

THE LESSONS OF DRESSAGE

Dressage" or rather the training of lessons does not serve the rider, but the gymnasticization of the horse. It is therefore not only challenged, but above all encouraged. Inconsistencies or even problems can be solved through different exercises. In dressage, these lessons are shown during a test according to the class. We will look at the necessary aids and the correct execution of the most common lessons.

When **backing up,** the horse moves backwards diagonally in double time. The horse makes kicks and not steps as usual. Normally a horse walks in four-beat time, so it places each hoof individually. When backing up, however, the horse walks in two-beat time, i.e. simultaneously to the front right and back left, then simultaneously to the front left and back right. This lesson requires the rider to have a balanced seat and the horse to be on the aids. To avoid mistakes, the exercise should be started from the ground. Timing is very important here, which is why attention must be paid to every movement of the horse. This lesson can be ridden from any gait. Once the horse has parried and is standing, you should first think forwards. As soon as the horse wants to take its first step in the shoulder, you can think backwards. Slightly relieve the horse's back to give it room to move backwards. Now increase the drive and give a half parade. Depending on the horse's footing, the driving and relieving aids should be increased or decreased. The goal is a collected and clearly off-foot horse.

The **short turn is** a hindquarters turn in which the horse turns 180 degrees around the hindquarters with the forehand. Important: The horse must not step forward, only sideways. The prerequisite is that the horse is collected and its hindquarters can bear weight.

The short turn is initiated by the rider giving a half parade to collect the horse. He then places it on the inside. The balance is then shifted to the inside, the outside leg begins to drive carefully and the direction is indicated with the inside hand. The outside leg must not be too far back during this process, as this would activate the hindquarters and the horse would go into a leg yield. Once the horse is back on the hoof, it is straightened.

Riding **medium trot and canter** gymnasticizes horses very well and strengthens the hindquarters in particular. This lesson shows how much the rider can influence the animal. It is often assumed that the horse only needs to move forward faster, but that is not the aim here. The aim is to increase the size of the strides and for the horse to actively under-stride with its hindquarters. To achieve this, the rider reinforces the driving aids and at the same time catches the horse in front again so that it steps towards the rider's hand. The prerequisite for this is that there is a constant contact and that the animal responds well to the rider's leg and weight aids.

The **collected trot and canter** show the opposite. The hindquarters take on more weight, the strides are shortened and there is a slightly longer suspension moment between the strides.

For many horses, the **outside canter is** difficult because they cannot balance themselves sufficiently. In most cases, they also lack the strength in their hindquarters to take the load. However, with a little practice, everything is possible. At the beginning, the horse is ridden in hand canter and then a hand change is introduced. A practical hoof beat figure for this is "turn out of the corner". Once you are on the new hand, you need to keep the horse on the old hand. This means that the inside leg remains behind as if it were the outside leg and the horse is still turned slightly to the outside. It is important to support the horse's balance as much as possible at . This will also show whether the horse is on the aids and in collection.

The **shoulder-in is** a great lesson to improve the horse's suppleness, balance and collection. The horse is positioned from the head to just behind the shoulders inwards so that it moves on a total of 3 hoof beats and is positioned at around 30 degrees to the boundaries of the arena or arena. However, it should not be bent too much. It is best to ride the shoulder-in from a circle. When approaching the long straight, the position is maintained, but the horse is driven straight along the rail with the inside rein. The outside rein can be opened slightly to give the horse room to move. It is important that the rider remains upright in the saddle. If he shifts his weight, he will throw the horse off balance. The shoulder-in can be ridden at the walk, trot and canter.

The **leg yield is a** good lesson, especially for beginners, to understand the interplay of weight, leg and rein aids, as these must be very well coordinated in order to master the exercise. Similar to the shoulder-in, the horse moves on several hooves. Here, each hoof is on one hoof beat, meaning that a total of four hoof beats are used. The horse is positioned at a maximum of 45 degrees. At the beginning, it can also be placed towards the rail, which can help with the lines. Otherwise, the rider usually turns onto the center or quarter line and from there changes through the arena. To do this, the rider shifts his weight to one side and drives with the inside leg, which the horse should yield to. It is important that the rider not only moves sideways but also forwards. The outer leg remains on the girth, keeping it there. The outer rein is used to set the boundaries. The inside rein is used to give position. However, the horse should not be bent, but should go straight. This is why this lesson is not part of the lateral movements.

The **traversal,** on the other hand, is one of the lateral movements. It is ridden at a collected trot or collected canter. As with leg yields and shoulder-in, the horse moves forward and sideways, but is bent and placed.

Depending on the level of difficulty, the horse either changes through the whole arena or, in higher classes, only through half the arena.

The lesson is introduced with half halts to collect the horse. When riding from the short side to the long side, the bend and position from the bend is maintained. The inside buttock is loaded, the inside leg drives and holds the horse in the bend, while the outside leg lies behind the girth and initiates the forward and sideways movement. The inside rein can be used to support the lateral movement. The outside rein has a limiting effect. A half traversal is only ridden to or from the centerline. In the zigzag traversal, the rider turns to the centerline and rides the traversal to the quarter line.

There the rider changes over and traverses over the center line to the quarter line on the other side. The rider changes again and then only rides to the centerline. The traversal ends there.

The traversal can also be ridden in canter. A flying change is performed at the changeover points.

Simple canter changes demand and promote the horse's permeability. The prerequisite for this is that the horse is able to parry calmly and fluently from canter to walk and can also canter from walk. Once this has been consolidated, the changes can be worked on. In the simple canter change, the horse is parried through from canter to walk and this is ridden through for approximately one horse length. The horse is first ridden straight and then switched to the other hand. The horse is then cantered again on this new hand. The best way to practise this is to "change through the circle" or "turn out of the corner". The "turn out of the corner" is ridden through in hand canter. One horse length before reaching the hoofbeat, the horse is parried through to walk and changed over. The horse is then cantered again on the new hand. The same procedure is followed on a circle. It is "changed out of the circle" and the horse is parried over X, repositioned and cantered again.

If the simple change works well, you can start working on the **flying change.** Suitable hoof beat figures here are also "change out of the circle", "turn out of the corner" and "change through the whole arena". Let's take the example of "change through the whole arena". The hoof beat figure is ridden in hand canter. X is the point at which the flying change is to take place. To start with, you can place a cavaletti on the point where you want to jump over as an aid. Then you can switch to a pole lying on the ground. If this also works, you can take it away and practise it without aids.

Series changes are only required from advanced level upwards. This is a series of flying canter changes. A distinction is made between single, double, triple and quadruple changes. In the single change, a flying change is performed at every canter jump. The horse remains straight. The double change takes place after every second canter jump. The triple changes take place after every third canter jump and the quadruple changes after every fourth canter jump. The greatest difficulty lies in maintaining the same tempo and rhythm.

The **renvers** can be used to ride a horse on the inside aids. The horse's body is directed inwards away from the rail on the long side. However, the horse is positioned towards the rail. The weight is applied uni-laterally in the direction of movement and the inside rein drives the hindquarters sideways. The inside rein limits and the outside rein points the direction.

The **piaffe is** a lesson that demands absolute collection, because the horse's trotting movement is so collected that the horse only moves forward minimally. The horse's hind hand steps far under the body. The hooves are lifted to the level of the fetlock head. The extent to which a horse lifts its hooves off the ground is called cadence.

The prerequisite is that the horse can bend its hip, knee and hock joints and carry itself. The biggest challenge here is to maintain the rhythm. The rider sits low in the saddle. His outer hand slows the forward movement, while the inner hand keeps the horse straight and upright. How much you have to push varies from horse to horse, but generally the leg is about half a hand's width behind the girth. It is driven alternately in time with the kicks in order to encourage the hindquarters to follow the same rhythm.

The **passage,** on the other hand, is also a collected trot movement, but the suspension phase between the steps is significantly extended. The passage is best initiated from the piaffe. The horse is still led back in trot. This means that the forward movement is intercepted at the front. However, the forward movement is not slowed down during the passage. The cadence of the piaffe should be maintained and supplemented by an extended suspension phase.

A **pirouette** can be ridden in walk, canter or as a piaffe. Not every horse is anatomically predisposed to perform this exercise perfectly. We will look at it using the example of the canter pirouette: Here, the horse's forehand moves in a small circle around the hindquarters. A full pirouette consists of six to eight canter jumps in which the horse turns once through 360 degrees. A half pirouette is just a 180 degree turn with three to four jumps.

To slowly but surely prepare horses for this, you should practise the shoulder-in canter on the long side. The traversal can also help in preparation. If the horse goes in a collected canter, the work can begin. The weight aid is shifted strongly to the inside. The inside leg and inside rein ensure bending and position. The horse is guided and limited by the outside leg and the outside rein. Every canter jump should be ridden as if you were giving an aid to canter. It is important that the interruption of the pirouette is also trained. It is not easy to straighten out from such a strong sideways movement and requires a high degree of tact and permeability.

DRESSAGE CLASSES

Dressage is divided into different classes in order to differentiate the scope of performance. Even for young riders, for example, there are **lead rein and lunge competitions**. They form a separate class of equestrian competitions. This is followed by the **E dressage**. E means beginner and, as the name suggests, is intended to provide an introduction to dressage riding.

Everyone starts once and that is exactly what it is ideal for. From this class onwards, badge tests (e.g. riding badge seven) must be taken before the show to ensure that the rider meets the requirements. At beginner level in particular, the rider's ability and the horse's skills can be overestimated. Not only the practical riding of the lessons of a corresponding class is tested, but also the basic theoretical knowledge. The test is intended to demonstrate mastery of all basic gaits on hoof paces such as circles, serpentines or half-passes. Most tests in class E are ridden in a section. This demonstrates that the rider has their horse under control and whether they have a feeling for working with other riders. The test should be harmonious and synchronized. The rider's seat, the horse's rideability and the overall impression conveyed during the test are assessed. In principle, the test only lasts three minutes, but these three minutes require concentration and can be very strenuous.

This is followed by the **A dressage test**. The A stands for beginner, but does not mean that it will be easy. The class builds on what is required in E dressage. In addition, there are slightly more demanding exercises such as backing up, which is intended to show that the horse is collected. This also allows the judges to see whether the rider has a feel for the aids they can give through their seat. Another lesson is "letting the reins out of the hand". The judges want to see whether the horse's muscles are relaxed or whether it is tense. The over-reining shows whether the horse is on the right aids. Furthermore, not only the basic gaits are tested, but also the reinforcement for the medium trot and medium canter. This shows whether the rider has control over the horse and can influence the speed at any time. In addition, the rider should be able to reduce/expand the arena and ride with precision. Here too, horse and rider should present a harmonious picture.

Even if it is described as an easy class, **L dressage is** anything but easy. In addition to the requirements from class A, there is also collection. The horse should actively step under with its hindquarters. This means that not only the increased trot and canter must be shown, but also the collected trot and canter. The transitions should be clearly recognizable. Voltes at the trot and the hindquarters turn (also: short turn) are also included. This enables the judges to recognize whether the horse can be bent and placed and whether it is standing correctly on the aids. The outside canter should be shown to determine whether the rider has collected the horse. In general, the test consists of many hoof beat figures that include changes of hand. For example, changes out of the circle or turns out of the corner.

This is followed by the **M dressage test**. M stands for medium level and these are already at the professional level. In the aforementioned classes, the arena was always 20 by 40 meters. In medium dressage, the size can be 20 by 60 meters. The lessons are always ridden on a curb bit. In addition to the lessons of the previous classes, more lateral movements, such as the traversal and the shoulder-in, are shown. Reinforced trot and canter are also required. Changes of tempo, reinforcement and collection should therefore be safely mastered. The first flying changes are also tested in preparation for the next higher classes.

Class S, the most difficult of all. It is also usually ridden on a curb bit and lasts between five and six minutes. The most demanding variations of the lessons are required here.

This means that not only the traversal should be shown, but also the zigzag traversal and traversal shifts in canter. The piaffe, passage, renvers, canter changes, about-turns and the pirouette are also to be shown. Internationally, a distinction is made between the St. Georg, the Grand Prix and the Grand Prix Special.

The crowning glory of dressage is the freestyle, also known as freestyle dressage. The same equestrian performance of the movements applies, but these should be presented to music. A proper choreography is therefore developed. The rider decides for himself and his horse which lessons he chooses and in which order they are performed. The choice of music can range from classical to pop.

The tests are scored on a scale from zero to ten. Zero means not performed and 10 means that the ride was excellent. However, intermediate marks, such as 7.8 or 8.3, are also possible. In this way, the judges give a weighting to the score. The overall mark is made up of individual marks from the lessons. If a rider falls, 2.0

points are deducted. A ride below 5.0 will no longer be placed.

From elementary class upwards, there is not just one judge, but three. The score is then not a grade, but a number of points.

As already mentioned, regardless of the different classes, attention is always paid to the overall picture in every competition. Rider and horse should work together in harmony. Understanding the nature of the horse, a balanced seat and correct aids are crucial for this.